OBERLIN COLLEGE LIBRARY
BULLETIN NO. 5

TRIAL

BIBLIOGRAPHY AND OUTLINE

OF LECTURES ON THE

Financial History of the United States

BY

E. L. BOGART.

AND

W. A. RAWLES.

TRIAL

BIBLIOGRAPHY AND OUTLINE

OF LECTURES ON THE

Financial History of the United States

BY

ERNEST L. BOGART, A.M., PH.D.
Associate Professor of Economics and Sociology, Oberlin College

AND

WILLIAM A. RAWLES, A.M.
Assistant Professor of Economics, Indiana University

GREENWOOD PRESS, PUBLISHERS
NEW YORK

Originally published in 1901
by The News Printing Company

First Greenwood Reprinting 1969

SBN 8371-2157-4

PRINTED IN UNITED STATES OF AMERICA

CHAPTER I. THE COLONIAL PERIOD.

1. The Currency.

(i) Commodities.

BOOKS.—W. B. Weeden, *Soc. and Econ. Hist. of New England* (see index, "Money"); Woodford, *Wampum;* J. B. Felt, *Mass. Currency*, p. 20; H. White, *Money and Banking*, p. 4; C. J. Bullock, *Monetary History of U. S.*, ch. ii.; P. A. Bruce, *Economic History of Virginia;* W. Z. Ripley, *Financial History of Virginia;* J. T. Scharf, *History of Maryland;* W. F. DeKnight, *Currency and Loans;* B. Fernow, *Currency of New York;* J. V. La McMahon, *History of Maryland;* C. H. Douglas, *Financial History of Massachusetts;* McCready, *South Carolina.*

PERIODICALS.—W. B. Weeden, *Indian Money*, J. H. U. Studies, 2d Series, VIII.-IX.; S. W. Rosendale, *Wampum Currency*, Sound Currency III. p. 483; H. Bronson, *Connecticut Currency*, N. H. Hist. Soc. Papers I.

SOURCES.—*Documents of Colonial History of New York*, I.; E. B. O'Callaghan, *Laws of New Netherlands;* W. Douglass, *Discourse; Coll. Mass. Hist. Soc.*

(ii) Metallic Money.

BOOKS.—D. K. Watson, *History of American Coinage*, ch. i.; S. S. Crosby, *Coins in America;* J. H. Hickcox, *American Coinage;* J. B. Felt, *Massachusetts Currency;* C. J. Bullock, *Monetary History*, ch. iii.; C. H. Douglas, *Financial History of Massachusetts*, sec. 28-9; W. Z. Ripley, *Financial History of Virginia;* S. L. Adler, *Money of American Colonies;* R. Chalmers, *Colonial Currency;* P. A. Bruce, *Economic History of Virginia*, II.; W. Bradford, *Plymouth Plantation;* A. Delmar, *Money and Civilization*, and *Money in America;* B. Fernow, *Currency of New York;* B. R. Carroll, *South Carolina*, II.; J. H. Hickcox, *Bills of Credit;* J. R. McCulloch, *Dictionary of Commerce;* H. Phillips, *Paper Currency;* E. Potter and S. S. Rider, *Money of Rhode*

Island; R. Ruding, *Coinage of Great Britain;* J. T. Scharf, *History of Maryland*, II.; W. R. Shepherd, *Government in Pennsylvania;* S. Smith, *History of New Jersey;* D. K. Watson, *Annals of Philadelphia;* W. M. Gouge, *Paper Money and Banking in U.S.*

PERIODICALS.—H. Bronson, *Connecticut Currency;* W. G. Sumner, *Coin Shilling of Massachusetts*, Yale Rev. VII. 247, 405; C. H. Swan, Jr., *Spanish Silver Dollar in Massachusetts*, Sound Currency, VI. 73–80.

SOURCES.—J. Ashley, *British Colonies;* J. Winthrop, *New England*, I.; B. Franklin, *Works*, III. 426, IV. 84, and *passim;* J. Hutchinson, *History of Massachusetts;* J. Belknap, *History of New Hampshire;* H. Williamson, *History of North Carolina;* D. Ramsay, *History of South Carolina;* W. Smith, *History of New York;* T. Jefferson, *Writings*, VII.; J. Wright, *American Negotiator;* W. Douglass, *Discourse.*

(iii) Bank Paper Money.

BOOKS.—J. E. T. Rogers, *First Nine Years of the Bank of England*, 1–88; J. H. Trumbull, *First Essays at Banking;* J. B. Felt, *Massachusetts Currency*, 47 ff.; W. B. Weeden, *New England* (see index, "Banks"). W. G. Sumner, *History of Banking in U. S.*, ch. i.; C. H. Douglass, *History of Massachusetts*, 41–7, 121–131; J. Winsor, *Narrative and Critical History of America*, V. 170–176; H. White, *Money and Banking*, 248–258; J. J. Knox, *United States Notes*, 1 ff.; C. J. Bullock, *Monetary History of the United States*, 29–32; Phillips, *Colonial and Continental Paper Currency*, I. 27 ff.; J. J. Knox, in Lalor's Cyclopedia, I. 204–6.

MASS.—C. H. Douglass, *Financial History of Mass.*, ch. iv.; J. B. Felt, *Mass. Currency;* J. K. Hosmer, *Samuel Adams*, 31–2, 252.

CONN.—H. Bronson, *Conn. Currency.*

RH. IS.—E. Potter and S. S. Rider, *Paper Money of Rh. Is.;* S. G. Arnold, *History of Rh. Is.*, II. 39 (see index, "Banks"); F. G. Bates, *Rh. Is. and the Formation of the Union*, Col. Univ. Studies, X. No. 2.

NEW YORK.—J. H. Hickcox, *Bills of Credit:* B. Fernow, *Coins and Currency of New York;* H. White, *New York's Colonial Currency*, Sound Currency, V. 50–64; T. Roosevelt, *Gouverneur Morris*, 20–1.

SO. CAR.—D. Ramsay, *History of So. Car.*, II.; E. L. Whitney, *The Government of So. Car.;* B. R. Carroll, *Hist. Collections of So. Car.; So. Car.'s First Paper Money*, Sound Currency, V. 34–45.

NO. CAR.—*History of No. Car.*, II.; C. J. Bullock, *Monetary History of U. S.*, 125–204.

NEW. H.—C. J. Bullock, *Monetary History of U. S.*, 207–273.

NEW JERSEY.—I. S. Mulford, *History of N. J.*

GA.—W. B. Stevens, *Hist. of Ga.*, I. 399.

PENN.—W. R. Shepherd, *Proprietary Government in Penn.*, 4–27; T. K. Worthington, *Finances of Penn.*, Pub. Am. Econ. Assoc., II. 136 ff.; C. W. MacFarlane, *Penn. Paper Currency*, Annals of Amer. Acad., VIII. 50–126.

MD.—J. T. Scharf, *History of Md.*, II. 37.

VA.—W. Z. Ripley, *Financial History of Va.*

PERIODICALS.—L. C. Root, *New England Bank Currency*, Sound Currency, II. No. 13, p. 2–3; C. F. Dunbar, *Notes on Early Banking Schemes* (in England), Quart. Journ. Econ., II. 482–490; A. M. Davis, *Currency Discussion in Mass. in the Eighteenth Century*, Quart. Journ. Econ., XI. 70, 136; A. M. Davis, *A Connecticut Land Bank of the Eighteenth Century*, Quart. Jour. Econ. XIII. 70.

SOURCES.—T. Hutchinson, *History of Massachusetts*, II. 188; W. Douglass, *Discourse.*

(iv) Government Paper Money.

BOOKS.—C. J. Bullock, *Monetary History of the United States*, 32–59; H. White, *Money and Banking*, 120–134; J. Winsor, *Narrative and Critical History of America*, V. 170–176, 328; J. B. Felt, *Massachusetts Currency*, 62; W. G. Sumner, *History of American Currency;* W. B. Weeden, *New England* (see index "Money"); Phillips, *Colonial and Continental Paper Money*, I.; J. H. Trumbull, *First Essays at Banking;* H. Phillips, *Historical Sketches of American Paper Currency;* E. B. Greene, *The Provincial Governor*, 163–173; G. Bancroft, *A Plea for the Constitution*, Part I.; W. F. DeKnight, *Currency and Loans*, 6–11.

PERIODICALS.—C. W. MacFarlane, *Penn. Paper Currency*, Annals, VIII., 50–126; A. M. Davis, *Currency Discnssion in Mass. in the Eighteenth Century*, Quart. Journ. Econ., XI., 70, 136; Mag. of Amer. Hist., II., 627; R. M. Breckenridge, *Paper Currencies of New France*, Jour. Pol. Econ., I., 406.

SOURCES.—W. Douglass, *Discourse;* W. Douglass, *Summary;* T. Paine, *Writings*, II., 181; Morris, *Papers*, 213–226, 250, 270, 274, 310, 314–320; T. Hutchinson, *History of Mass.*, II.; G. R.

Minot, *History of Mass.*, I.; J. Belknap, *History of New Hampshire*, II., 425; *Works of Franklin*, III., IV.; P. Webster, *Political Essays;* R. Proud, *History of Penn.;* J. Witherspoon, *Works*, IX.; *Statutes of So. Car.*, II., IV.; *Papers of N. H.*, III., V.; *Col. Recs. of No. Car.*, II., IV.; J. Iredell, *Laws of No. Car.; Documents of New York*, VI.; *Records of Rh. Is.; Coll. Mass. Hist. Soc.*

2. Colonial Taxation and Administration of Finances.

BOOKS.—R. T. Ely, *Taxation in Amer. States and Cities*, 105–114; J. B. McMaster, *History of Amer. People*, I., 588 ff.; W. G. Sumner, *Financier and Finances of Amer. Revolution*, I., 11–34.

NEW ENGLAND.—C. H. Douglas, *Financial History of Mass.;* F. A. Wood, *History of Taxation in Vermont*, Col. Univ. Studies, IV., 311; F. R. Jones, *History of Taxation in Conn.*, J. H. U. Studies, XIV., No. 8; W. B. Weeden, *Soc. and Econ. History of New England* (see index, "Taxes").

MIDDLE COLONIES.—J. C. Schwab, *History of N. Y. Property Tax*, Pub. Amer. Econ. Assn., V., 363 ff; T. K. Worthington, *Finances of Penn.*, Pub. Amer. Econ. Assn., II., 126 ff.

SOUTHERN COLONIES.—W. Z. Ripley, *Financial History of Va.;* T. S. Adams, *Taxation in Md.*, J. H. U. Studies, XVIII., 26–8; *Maryland Tax Commission's Report*, 1888; L. F. Schmeckebier, *Taxation in Ga.*, J. H. U. Studies, XVIII., 220.

PERIODICALS.—E. R. A. Seligman, *Income Tax in Amer. Colonies and States*, Pol. Sci. Quart., X.; C. F. Dunbar, *Some Precedents Followed by Alex. Hamilton*, Quart. Journ. Econ., Oct., 1888.

CHAPTER II.

THE REVOLUTION AND THE CONFEDERATION, 1775–1789.

1. Revenues.

(1) Continental Paper Money.

BOOKS.—*American Almanac*, 1830, pp. 182–3; G. Bancroft, *History of U. S.*, VI., 20, 167; G. Bancroft, *Plea for the Constitution*, Part II.; F. G. Bates, *Rh. Is. and the Formation of the Union*,

Col. Univ. Studies, X., No. 2; A. S. Bolles, *Financial History of U. S.*, I.; Bolles, in *Lalor's Cyclopedia*, II., 189–208; S. Breck, *Continental Paper Money;* H. Bronson, *Conn. Currency;* C. J. Bullock, *Monetary History of U. S.*, ch. v.; C. J. Bullock, *Finances of U. S.*, 1775–1789; W. M. Gouge, *Short History of Paper Money and Banking;* R. Hildreth, *History of U. S.*, III., ch. xlvi. (see index "Paper Money"); B. W. Holt, *Continental Currency*, Sound Currency, V., 81–112; J. J. Knox, *United States Notes;* O. G. Libby, *Geographical Distribution of the Vote on the Federal Constitution*, Univ. of Wisc., Bull. in Econ., Pol. Sci., and Hist., Series I., No. 1; J. B. McMaster, *History of Amer. People*, I., chs. ii,–iv.; Phillips, *Continental Paper Money;* Phillips, *Paper Currency of the Revolution;* E. A. Ross, *Sinking Funds*, Pub. Amer. Econ. Assn., VII.; J. W. Shuckers, *Finances and Paper Money of the Revolutionary War;* W. G. Sumner, *History of American Currency;* W. G. Sumner, *Financier and Finances of the American Revolution;* H. White, *Money and Banking*, 134–148; W. F. De-Knight, *Currency and Loans*, 12–17; J. Winsor, *America*, VII. 81; J. Elliot, *The Funding System;* W. B. Weeden, *New England*, II., ch. ii.; F. A. Walker, *Making of the Nation*, 18; H. C. Lodge, *Geo. Washington*, I., 258–262; S. H. Gay, *James Madison*, 21; T. Roosevelt, *Gouverneur Morris*, 20, 21, 32; J. A. Stevens, *Albert Gallatin*, 171; H. C. Lodge, *Alexander Hamilton*, 26–7; G. Pellew, *John Jay*, 100.

SOURCES.—*Amer. State Papers, Finance*, I. and V.; *Journals of Congress; Secret Journals of Congress;* P. Webster, *Political Essays;* P. Force, *American Archives;* Reed's *Reed*, II., 41; Lincoln, *Shay's Rebellion*, in A. B. Hart's *American History Told by Contemporaries*, III., 191; Varnum, *Case of Trevett against Weeden.*

See also authorities quoted under I, 1, (iv).

(ii) Loans.

BOOKS.—G. Bancroft, *History of U. S.*, IV.–V.; R. A. Bayley, *National Loans of U. S.*, Tenth Census, VII. 10–21; A. S. Bolles, *Financial History of U. S.*, I. 223, 267–359; C. J. Bullock, *Finances of U. S ;* H. Doniol, *Histoire de la Participation de la France à l'Établissement des États Unis d'Amérique;* Elliot, *Funding System*, 59–61, 91, 92; E. E. Hale, *Franklin in France;* T. Pitkin, *History of U. S.*, II. ch. xvi., xvii.; J. Schouler, *History of U. S.*, I.; W. F. De Knight, *Currency and Loans*, 17–20, 29–32; W. G. Sumner, *Financier and Finances of American Revolution*,

I. 164; J. T. Morse, *Benjamin Franklin*, 306-337; S. H. Gay, *James Madison*, 28; T. Roosevelt, *Gouveneur Morris*, 79-88; G. Pellew, *John Jay*, 100-1, 118-120.

PERIODICALS.—J. Fiske, Atlantic Mo., July, 1886.

SOURCES.—*American State Papers*, *Finance*, III. and IV.; *Journals of Congress*, VII.-XIII., *passim; Secret Journals of Congress;* A. Gallatin, *Writings*, III. 121-7; A. B. Hart, *American History told by Contemporaries*, III. 255.

(iii) Taxes and Requisitions.

BOOKS.—Bolles, *Financial History of U. S.*, I.; Bullock, *Finances of U. S.;* J. Elliot, *Report on the Funding System in the U. S. and Great Britain* (Exec. Doc., 28 Cong., 1st sess., No. 15); R. T. Ely, *Taxation in American States and Cities*, 105-115; R. Hildreth, *History of U. S.*, III. (see index, "Requisitions"); W. Hill, *First Stages of Tariff Policy of U. S.*, Pub. Amer. Econ. Ass'n, VIII.; J. T. Morse, *Life of Alex. Hamilton*, Reports of 1785 and 1790; W. G. Sumner, *Alex. Hamilton;* W. G. Sumner, *Financier of American Revolution;* G. T. Curtis, *Constitutional History of U. S.*, II. 104, 124; J. Story, *Commentaries on the Constitution*, §254.

SOURCES.—*American State Papers*, *Finance*, I.; Gallatin, *Writings*, III.; *The Federalist*, No. XXX.; *Journals of Congress; Secret Journals of Congress.*

(iv) Miscellaneous.

BOOKS.—Bolles, *Financial History of U. S.*, I., 49; H. B. Adams, *Maryland's Influence upon the Land Cessions to the U. S.*, J. H. U. Studies, III., No. 1; Bullock, *Finances of the U. S.;* Elliot, *Funding System;* T. Donaldson, *The Public Domain;* McMaster, *History of American People*, I.; Ross, *Sinking Funds*, Pub. Amer. Econ. Assn., VII.; J. Fiske, *Critical Period*, ch. iv.; S. Sato, *History of the Land Question in the U. S.*, J. H. U. Studies, IV.; R. A. Bayley, *National Loans of U. S.*, Tenth Census, VII.; E. E. Hale, *Franklin in France;* T. Pitkin, *History of U. S.*, I. and II.; Sumner, *Financier and Finances of the American Revolution*, I., 101.

SOURCES.—Gallatin, *Writings*, III.; *Journals of Congress; Secret Journals of Congress.*

2. Expenditures of the Government.

BOOKS.—Bolles, *Financial History of U. S.*, I. 348–357; Bullock, *Finances of U. S.;* J. Elliott, *Report on the Funding System* (Exec. Doc., 28th Cong., 1st sess., No. 15); R. Hildreth, *History of U. S.*, III. (see index, "Expenditures and Estimates"); H. C. Lodge, *George Washington*, I. 258; S. H. Gay, *James Madison*, 22.

SOURCES.—*Diplomatic Correspondence of the American Revolution*, VI.; *American State Papers, Finance* I.; Gallatin, *Writings*, III.; Jefferson, *Works*, IX.; Hamilton's Report of 1790, reprinted in *Bankers' Magazine*, XIV.

3. The Administration of the Finances.

BOOKS.—Bolles, *Financial History of U. S.*, I. 9; Bullock, *Finances of U. S.;* Hildreth, *History of U. S.*, III.; Sumner, *Financier and Finances of the American Revolution*, I. 261, 280; II. 64, 95, 102, 131; Bancroft, *History of U. S.*, V.; H. C. Adams, *Public Debts;* J. C. Guggenheimer, *Development of the Executive Departments*, 1775–1789; L. Lewis, *History of the Bank of North America;* J. Sparks, *Gouverneur Morris*, I., ch. xvi., xvii.; J. C. Hamilton, *Life of Alex. Hamilton*, I., ch. xi., xiii.., xv.; T. Roosevelt, *Gouverneur Morris*, 99–108; Curtis, *Constitution*, I. 172; J. T. Morse, *Benjamin Franklin*, 304–6; Lodge, *George Washington*, I. 259, 312; III. 105–6; Stevens, *Albert Gallatin*, 171–4, 248–50; Pellew, *John Jay*, 118; Roosevelt, *Gouverneur Morris*, 89–94; Lodge, *Alexander Hamilton*, 26–29, 39.

SOURCES.—*Journals of Congress; Secret Journals of Congress;* Alexander Hamilton, *Works*, I.; Jas. Madison, *Papers*, I.; Washington, *Writings* (Sparks ed.), VIII., IX.; *Mass. Hist. Soc. Proc.*, V. 470.

CHAPTER III.

THE FEDERALIST ADMINISTRATION, 1789-1801.

1. The Financial Situation in 1789. Analysis of Hamilton's Report on the Public Credit.

BOOKS.—Bolles, *Financial History of U. S.*, II., 1–33; F. C. Howe, *Taxation in U. S. under Internal Revenue System;* J. W.

Kearny, *Sketch of American Finances*, ch. i.; Lodge, *Alex. Hamilton*, 85-95; Lodge, *Washington*, II., 107; Morse, *Thomas Jefferson*, 88; Stevens, *Albert Gallatin*, 74, 243.

SOURCES.—Hamilton's Report on the Public Credit, in *Works* (1885), II., 47, 285, 305; in *American State Papers, Finance*, I., 15-25; in *Annals of Congress*, 1789-91, II., 1982, 2042; and in MacDonald's *Select Documents*, 46; *Reports on the Finances*, 1837, pp. 17-27.

2. The Funding of the Revolutionary Debt.

BOOKS.—Bolles, *Financial History of U. S.*, II., ch. iii.; DeKnight, *Currency and Loans*, 33; McMaster, *History of American People*, I., 568-584; Hildreth, vol. IV. (see index "Debt"); J. W. Kearny, *Sketch of Amer. Finances*, ch. i.; Lodge, *Alex. Hamilton*, ch. v. and vi.; Morse, *Alex. Hamilton*, I., 287; T. Pitkin, *History of U. S.*, II., 538; Schouler, *History of U. S.*, I., 130; Lodge, *Washington*, II., 107-8; Lodge, *Alex. Hamilton*, 115-127; Morse, *Thomas Jefferson*, 88-91; Stevens, *Albert Gallatin*, 174-5; Gay, *James Madison*, 144-152.

PERIODICALS.—C. F. Dunbar, *Some Precedents Followed by Hamilton*, Quart. Journ. Econ., III., 32; W. P. Sterns, *International Indebtedness of U. S. in 1789*, Journ. Pol. Econ., VI., 27; W. P. Sterns, *Beginning of American Financial Independence*, Journ. Pol. Econ., VI. 187.

SOURCES.—*U. S. Statutes*, I. 138, 178; Dunbar's *Laws*, 10, 18; *American State Papers, Finance*, I. 15-37, 76-81, 90-91, 479; *Annals of Congress*, I.-III.; *Annual Report of Sec. of Treas.*, 1837; Gallatin, *Sketch of the Finances*, in Writings, III, 69, 107; Jefferson, *Works*, IX. 91-96; *American State Papers, Misc.*, I. 69; *Laws of U. S.*, 3; Hamilton, *Works*, III., IV., VI., 632-651; Hamilton, *History of the Republic*.

3. The Redemption of the Debt, and the Sinking Fund.

BOOKS.—H. C. Adams, *Public Debts*, Pt. II. ch. iii., v.; Pt. III. ch. ii.; Bolles, *Financial History of the U. S.*, II. ch. iv.; J. Elliott, *Funding System* (Exec. Doc., 28th Cong., 1st sess., No. 15), 345, 429, 900; R. Hildreth, *History of U. S.*, VI (see index, "Sinking Fund"); Kearny, *Sketch of American Finances*, ch. i.-ii.; Lodge. *Alex. Hamilton*, 546; Ross, *Sinking Funds*, Pub. Amer.

Econ. Ass'n, VII.; J. A. Porter, *City of Washington*, J. H. U. Studies, III.; Lodge, *Alex. Hamilton*, 92–3; Stevens, *Albert Gallatin*, 176; T. Pitkin, *Statistical View of U. S.*, ch. ix.

SOURCES.—*U. S. Statutes*, I. 186, 281, 433; Dunbar's *Laws*, 20, 32, 35; *American State Papers*, *Finance*, I. 176, 320, 381, 404; Alex. Hamilton, *Works*, II. 473; *Laws of U. S.*, 11; MacDonald, *Select Documents*, 61.

4. Revenue Measures.

(i) Imposts and Tonnage Duties.

BOOKS.—H. C. Adams, *Taxation in U. S., 1789–1816*, J. H. U. Studies, II. 14–30; Bolles, *Financial History of U. S.*, II., Bk. 1, ch. vi.; Bk. 3, ch. viii.; J. D. Goss, *History of Tariff Administration in U. S.*, Col. Univ. Studies, I.; W. Hill, *First Stages of Tariff Policy of U. S.*, Pub. Amer. Econ. Ass'n, VIII., ch. iv.; Hildreth, *History of U. S.*, VI. (see index, "Tariff" and "Imposts"); McMaster, *History of the American People*, I. 544–552; Morse, *Alex. Hamilton*, I. 348; Schouler, *History of the U. S.*, I. 86, 187, 354; Sumner, *Financier and Finances of the American Revolution*, II., ch. xxxi.–xxxii.; F. W, Taussig, *Tariff History of the U. S.*, 8–17; F. W. Taussig, *State Papers and Speeches on the Tariff*, ch. i.; J. L. Bishop, *History of American Manufactures*, II. 13–17; Kearny, *Sketch of American Finances*, ch. i.–ii.; G. S. White, *Memoir of Samuel Slater*, ch. i.–iv.; J. Elliott, *Funding System;* Fiske, *History of U. S.* (see index, "Tariff"); Walker, *Making of Nation*, 84; Lodge, *Washington*, II. 112–115; Kelley, *Tariff Acts under the Confederacy*, Pol. Sci. Quart. II.

SOURCES.—*U. S. Statutes*, I. 24, 180, 190, 259, 390, 411, 533; II. 84; MacDonald, *Select Documents*, 98.

(ii) Internal Taxation, and the Whiskey Rebellion.

BOOKS.—H. C. Adams, *Taxation in U. S., 1789–1816*, J. H. U. Studies, II.; Bolles, *Financial History of U. S.*, II., Bk. 1, ch. vi.; Hildreth, *History of U. S.*, VI. (see index, "Taxes"); Boutwell, *Direct and Excise Taxation in U. S.;* H. M. Brackinridge, *History of the Western Insurrection;* W. Findley, *History of Whiskey Insurrection;* R. T. Ely, *Taxation in American States and Cities*, ch. ii.; F. C. Howe, *Taxation in U. S. under Internal Revenue System;* Morse, *Alex. Hamilton*, II., ch. iv.; McMaster, *History of American People*, II. 189–203; J. Schouler, *History of U. S.*

(see index, "Revenue"); *Lalor's Cyclopedia*, I. 809; II. 573-5; Kearny, *Sketch of American Finances*, ch. i.-ii.; Walker, *Making of Nation*, 86, 125; Lodge, *Washington*, II. 123; Lodge, *Alex. Hamilton*, 95-6, 127; Stevens, *Albert Gallatin*, 175.

PERIODICALS.—C. F. Dunbar, *The Direct Tax of 1861*, Quart. Journ. Econ. III. 436-442.

SOURCES.—*U. S. Statutes*, I. 373, 527, 597; Gallatin, *Writings*, III. 1-67; Hamilton, *Works*, III. 297.

5. The First United States Bank.

BOOKS.—Bolles, *Financial History of the U. S.*, II. ch. vii.-viii.; Clarke and Hall, *Legislative and Documentary History of the Bank of the U. S.*, ch. ii.; Elliott, *Funding System*, 213, 296; C. A. Conant, *History of Modern Banks of Issue*, 288-292: J. J. Knox, *History of Banking in U. S.*, 35; Hildreth, *Banks, Banking and Paper Currencies*, ch. xv.; McMaster, *History of the American People*, II. 28-41; H. S. Randall, *Thomas Jefferson*, I. ch. xv.; White, *Money and Banking*, 258-270; Sumner, *History of American Currency*, 55-61; Sumner, *History of Banking in the U. S.*, ch. iii.; Sumner, *Alex. Hamilton*, ch. x., xi.; DeKnight, *Currency and Loans*, 21; Lodge, *Alex. Hamilton*, 98-102; Morse, *Thomas Jefferson*, 106-7; Stevens, *Albert Gallatin*, 175, 250-2.

PERIODICALS.—L. C. Root, *First U. S. Bank*, Sound Currency, IV., No. 7.

SOURCES.—Hamilton's Report on a National Bank, in *Works*, III. 125; in *American State Papers, Finance*, I. 67-76; in *Annals of Congress*, 1789-91, II. 2031, 2082; in MacDonald's *Select Documents*, 67-76, 81-98; and in Hart, *American History Told by Contemporaries*, III., 276; *American State Papers, Finance*, I. 67, 223, 275; *U. S. Statutes*, I. 191; Dunbar's *Laws*, 22; *Annual Report of Comptroller of Currency*, 1876, 6-11; Jefferson, *Works*, VII. 555 (also in MacDonald's *Select Documents*, 76); Hamilton, *Works*, IV. 104; Madison, *Works*, I. 525, 528-30; *Annals of Congress*, 1789-91, II, 2312, 2375; Benton's *Abridgment of Debates*, I.

6. The Coinage System.

BOOKS.—Bolles, *Financial History of U. S.*, II., ch. viii.; McMaster, *History of the American People*, I. 195; *Monetary Commission Report*, 108, 493-5; R. E. Preston, *History of the*

Monetary Legislation and Currency System of the U. S.; Sumner, *History of American Currency*, 54; White, *Money and Banking*, 29; D. K. Watson, *History of American Coinage;* DeKnight, *Currency and Loans*, 22; Sumner, *Financier and Finances of American Revolution*, II. 36; J. L. Laughlin, *History of Bimetallism in U. S.*, ch. ii.; Lodge, *Alex. Hamilton*, 105, 127–8; Stevens, *Albert Gallatin*, 175.

PERIODICALS.—Sumner, Amer. Hist. Rev., III. 607–619.

SOURCES.—*U. S. Statutes*, I. 246; Dunbar's *Laws*, 227, 253; *Annals of Congress*, 1789-1791, II. 2060; Hamilton, *Works*, III. 231.

7. General Estimate of the Federalist Administration.

BOOKS.—H. Adams, *Life of Gallatin*, 267–9; Bolles, *Financial History of U. S.*, II. 175; Hildreth, *History of U. S.*, II. 414; IV. 152–176, 206–229, 252–267, 536–538; Morse, *Alex. Hamilton*, I. 370; Schouler, *History of U. S.*, II. 63; McMaster, *History of the American People*, II., 22; Lodge, *Alex. Hamilton*, 94, 131–3, 228, 242; Stevens, *Albert Gallatin*, 69, 106–7, 176–8, 184–5; Roosevelt, *Gouverneur Morris*, 279–280.

SOURCES.—Gallatin, *Writings*, III.

CHAPTER IV.

THE REPUBLICAN ADMINISTRATION, 1801–1812.

1. The Revenue System.

BOOKS.—H. Adams, *Life of Gallatin*. 267–274, 292–297; H. Adams, *History of U. S.*, I. 239, 272; II. 75, 135; III. 210; V. 178; H. C. Adams, *Taxation in U. S.*, J. H. U. Studies, II. 57; Bolles, *Financial History of U. S.*, II., ch. xii.; Hildreth, *History of U. S.*, V. 422, 444; Schouler, *History of U. S.*, II. 21, 70–72; Morse, *Thomas Jefferson*, 237–8; Stevens, *Albert Gallatin*, 186–215, 218–223, 225–230.

SOURCES.—*U. S. Statutes*, II. 148, 291, 299, 769; Gallatin, *Writings*, III.

2. The Payment of the Revolutionary Debt, and the Sinking Fund.

BOOKS.—H. Adams, *Life of Gallatin*, 267–274, 292–297: H. Adams, *History of U. S.*, I. 272, IV. 148, 345; H. C. Adams, *Public Debts*, 162, 167, 176, 225, 266–7; H. C. Adams, *Taxation in U. S.*, J. H. U. Studies, II. 54; Bayley, *National Loans of U. S.* Tenth Census, VII., Part I., 339–342, 414–417; Bolles, *Financial History of U. S.*, II., ch. xii.; DeKnight, *Currency and Loans*, 42–45; Kearny, *Sketch of American Finances*, ch. ii.; Hildreth, *History of U. S.*, V. 422, 444; Ross, *Sinking Funds;* Stevens, *Albert Gallatin*, ch. vi.; Elliott, *Funding System*, 461.

SOURCES.—*U. S. Statutes*, II. 167; Dunbar's *Laws*, 49; Gallatin, *Writings;* Gallatin, *Report on Public Credit*, American State Papers, Finance, I. 746.

3. The Expiration of the Bank Charter.

BOOKS.—H. Adams, *History of U. S.*, I. 207, 327; V. 319, 329, 335; VII. 387–9; Bolles, *Financial History of U. S.*, II. 145–155; Clarke and Hall, *History of U. S. Bank*, 116; Elliot, *Funding System*, 513; Hildreth, *History of U. S.*, VI. 211, 228; Stevens, *Albert Gallatin*, 231, 252–60; White, *Money and Banking*, 263–270.

PERIODICALS.—*Accounts of First National Bank*, Quart. Journ, Econ., VI. 471; L. C. Root, *First U. S. Bank*, Sound Currency, IV., No. 7, pp. 8–11.

SOURCES.—*Annals of Congress*, XI.–XV.; Benton's *Abridgment of Debates*, II., III.; *American State Papers*, *Finance*, II. 301, 351, 451, 516.

CHAPTER V.

THE SECOND WAR WITH ENGLAND, 1812–1815.

1. Gallatin's War Policy.

BOOKS.—H. Adams, *Life of Gallatin*, 426–492 (450–455); H. Adams, *History of U. S.*, IV. 32, V. 357, VI. 156–9, 165–6, 235, 301, 446; H. C. Adams, *Public Debts*, 112; Hildreth, *History of U. S.*, VI. 106–7, 282–3, 388; Kearny, *Sketch of American Finances*, ch.

iii.; Schouler, *History of U. S.*, VI. 344-6; Stevens, *Albert Gallatin*, 210-212; G. M. Dallas, *Life and Writings of A. J. Dallas;* Elliot, *Funding System*, 623.

PERIODICALS.—H. C. Adams, *American War Financiering*, Pol. Sci. Quart., I.

SOURCES.—Gallatin, *Writings*, I. 501; Dallas, *Annual Report of Sec. of Treas.*, 1815, part I.; part II. 1-3; part III. 1.

2. War Loans.

BOOKS.—H. Adams, *History of U. S.*, VI. 206-7, VII. 44-5; H. Adams, *Albert Gallatin*, 477; H. C. Adams, *Public Debts*, 117; Bayley, *National Loans of U. S.*, Tenth Census, VII. 342-354, 417-430; Bolles, *Financial History of U. S.*, II. 219-241; DeKnight, *Currency and Loans*, 45-56; Kearny, *Sketch of American Finances*, ch. iii.; Elliot, *Funding System*, 623; Walker, *Making of Nation*, 255; G. M. Dallas, *Life and Writings of Dallas*, 234-243; Stevens, *Albert Gallatin*, 209-216.

SOURCES.—*Annual Report of Secy. of Treas.*, 1876, 24-53.

3. Treasury Notes.

BOOKS.—H. C. Adams, *Public Debts*, 117; Bayley, *National Loans of U. S.*, Tenth Census, VII. 342-5, 349, 351, 417-420, 424, 427-8, 483; Bolles, *Financial History of U. S.*, II. 261-283; DeKnight, *Currency and Loans*, 45-56; Knox, *U. S. Notes*, ch. iv.-v.; *Lalor's Cyclopedia*, III. 961-5; Stevens, *Albert Gallatin*, 207, 210; T. Pitkin, *Statistical View of U. S.*, ch. ix.

SOURCES.—*Annals of Congress*, XXIII.-XXVIII.; Benton, *Abridgment of Debates*, IV., V.; *American State Papers*, *Finance*, II. 564-6; Jefferson, *Works*, VI. 391; *Annual Report of Secy. of Treas.*, 1876, pp. 34-9; Niles, *Weekly Register*.

4. The Banks and the Suspension of Specie Payments.

BOOKS.—H. Adams, *History of U. S.*, VIII. 213-8; H. Adams, *Albert Gallatin;* Bolles, *Financial History of U. S.*, II. 261-278; W. M. Gouge, *History of Paper Money and Banking in the U.S.;* Hildreth, *History of U. S.*, 527, 591, 606-9, 630, 681; Kearny, *Sketch of American Finances*, ch. iii.; Schouler, *History of U. S.*, II. 415; Stevens, *Albert Gallatin*, 257-63; Sumner, *Andrew Jack-*

son, 48-9, 154; E. M. Shepard, *Martin VanBuren*, 287-8; C. Schurz, *Henry Clay*, I. 131-2; McMaster, *History of American People*, IV., ch. xxx.; Sumner, *History of Banking in U. S.*, chs. v.-x.

SOURCES.—Gallatin, *Writings*, III. 282-287; Gallatin, *Considerations on the Currency and Banking System of the U. S.;* Hart, *American History told by Contemporaries*, III. 441.

5. Internal Revenue and Direct Taxes.

BOOKS.—H. C. Adams, *Taxation in U. S.*, J. H. U. Studies, II.; Bolles, *Financial History of U. S.*, II. 242-260; F. C. Howe, *Taxation in U. S. under Internal Revenue System*, ch. ii.; Kearny, *Sketch of American Finances*, ch. iii.; *Lalor's Cyclopedia*, II. 575-6; Walker, *Making of Nation*, 256; Stevens, *Albert Gallatin*, 232-5; T. Pitkin, *Statistical View of U. S.*, ch. x.

SOURCES.—*U. S. Statutes*, III. 22, 39, 40, 42, 44, 77, 401 (Internal Revenue Acts), 53, 164, 255 (Direct Taxes Acts); *American State Papers, Finance*, II. 866; Jefferson, *Works;* Dallas, *Report on Finances*, State Papers, IX. 2.

CHAPTER VI.

RESUMPTION, PAYMENT OF THE DEBT, AND SECOND U. S. BANK, 1815-1834.

1. The Financial Policy of Dallas.

BOOKS.—H. Adams, *History of U. S.*, VIII. 243-4, 249-62, IX. 83-4, 100-106, 111-114, 140-1; Bolles, *Financial History of U. S.*, II. 278-283, 299-300, 303-334; Clarke and Hall, *History of Bank of U. S.*, 481, 519; G. M. Dallas, *Life and Writings of A. J. Dallas*, 129-139; Kearny, *Sketch of American Finances*, ch. iv.; Schouler, *History of U. S.* II., 416, 452; Elliot, *Funding System*, 623.

SOURCES.—*American State Papers, Finance*, III. 130-3; Dallas, *Finance Report*, 1815; Gallatin, *Writings*, III. 548.

2. Resumption of Specie Payments.

BOOKS.—H. Adams, *History of U. S.*, IX. 126–132; Kearny, *Sketch of American Finances*, ch. iv.; Hildreth, *Banks, Banking, and Paper Currencies*, chs. xvi.–xix.; Sumner, *History of American Currrncy*, 61–94; Knox, *U. S. Notes*, ch. v.; Stevens, *Albert Gallatin*, 267; Sumner, *Andrew Jackson*, 268; McMaster, *History of American People*, IV., ch. xxx.; Sumner, *History of Banking in U.S.*, chs. viii.–x.

SOURCES.—*U. S. Statutes*, III. 343; Dunbar's *Laws*, 95, 264; *American State Papers, Finance*, III. 130, IV. 769; Gallatin, *Writings*, III. 287–293; Niles, *Weekly Register*, XXIII. 89; Webster, *Works*, III. 48.

3. Payment of the Debt.

BOOKS.—Bolles, *Financial History of U. S.*, II. 303–316; Kearny, *Sketch of American Finances*, ch. iv.; Ross, *Sinking Funds*, Pub. Amer. Econ. Ass'n VII. 383; Elliot, *Sinking Funds*, 890; H. C. Adams, *Public Debts*.

SOURCES.—*U. S. Statutes*, III. 379; Dunbar's *Laws*, 97; *An. Report Sec'y Treasury*, 1835; Jackson's Message, 1835, in *Presidents' Messages* III. 160, 163.

4. Charter of Second U. S. Bank.

BOOKS.—Bolles, *Financial History of U. S.*, II. 317; Clarke and Hall, *History of U. S. Bank*, 481, 512, 519, 585, 613, 801; C. A. Conant, *History of Modern Banks of Issue*, 294–300; Hildreth, *History of U. S.*, VI. 463, 529, 541–3, 570, 589–90, 607–9, 650–4, 702; Elliot, *Funding System*, 590, 670; A. Johnston, *Second U. S. Bank*, Lalor's Cyclopedia, I. 201; Knox, *Second U. S. Bank*, Lalor's Cyclopedia, I. 208; Knox, *History of Banking in U. S.*, ch. iv., Stevens, *Albert Gallatin*, 265–7; Sumner, *Andrew Jackson*, 160–9, 266–271; McMaster, *History of American People*, IV. ch. xxx.; Sumner, *History of Banking in U. S.*, ch. xi.

PERIODICALS.—L. C. Root, *Second U. S. Bank*, Sound Currency, IV. Nos. 17–18.

SOURCES.—*U. S. Statutes* III. 266; Dunbar's *Laws*, 80, 257; *American State Papers, Finance*, II. 867, 891, III. 57; Gallatin, *Writings*, III. 236, 363, 389–90.

CHAPTER VII.

THE BANK CONTROVERSY, 1829-1842.

1. The Struggle Over the Re-charter.

BOOKS.—Bolles, *Financial History of U. S.*, II. 334-358; T. H. Benton, *Thirty Years' View*, I. 123, 158, 187, 205, 220-9, 232-265, 286-296, 371; C. Colton, *Henry Clay*, II. ch. i.; Conant, *History of Modern Banks of Issue*, 299; A. Johnston, in *La'or's Cyclopedia*, I. 201; Knox, *History of Banking*, ch. iv.; J. Parton, *Life of Andrew Jackson*, III. 260; Roosevelt, *Thomas H. Benton*, ch. vi.; C. Schurz, *Henry Clay*, II. ch. xiii., xv.; Sumner, *Andrew Jackson*, 277-81, 291-342; Sumner, *History of Banking*, ch. xii.; S. Tyler, *Memoir of Roger B. Taney*, I. ch. iii.; H. von Holst, *Constitutional History of U. S.* II. 31-51; H. A. Wise, *Seven Decades*, ch. vii.; White, *Money and Banking*, 287-313; G. T. Curtis, *Daniel Webster*, I. ch. xviii.; G. T. Curtis, *James Buchanan*, I. ch. x.-xi.; G. Tucker, *History of U. S.* IV. ch. xxvi.; C. H. Hunt, *Edward Livingston*, ch. xvi.; E. C. Mason, *The Veto Power*, §§ 55-59; E. Stanwood, *Presidential Elections*, ch. xiii.; Schouler, *History of U. S.* IV. ch. xiii., § 3; A. W. Young, *American Statesmen*, ch. xl., xlvi.

PERIODICALS.—R. C. H. Catterall, *Issues of the Second Bank of the U. S.*, Journ. Pol. Econ., V. 421.

SOURCES.—W. MacDonald, *Select Documents of U. S. History*, 238-9, 259-268; Gallatin, *Writings*, III. 390-406; Jackson, *Messages and Veto*, in *Messages and Papers of the Presidents*, II. 558, 576, III. 163, 251; Webster, *Works*, III. 391-447, IV. 82; *Ho. Reports*, 1831-2, No. 460 (Report of Investigating Committee of 1832); *Ho. Exec. Doc.*, 1833-4, No. 523 (Accounts of Bank); *Statesman's Manual*, 753, 767; Niles' *Weekly Register*, XLII. 315, 365; Dunbar's *Laws*, 266; *Register of Debates*, VI., VII.; Benton, *Abridgment of Debates*, X., XI.; J. Q. Adams, *Memoirs*, VII.; M. Van Buren, *Political Parties*, 311-362; Clarke and Hall, *History of U. S. Bank*, ch. vi.; J. A. Hamilton, *Reminiscences*, chs. vii.-viii.; D. Mallory, *Life and Speeches of Henry Clay*, II.; Henry Clay, *Private Correspondence*, chs. vii.-viii.

2. The Removal of the Deposits.

BOOKS.—Bolles, *Financial History of U. S.*, II. 334–358; Conant, *History of Modern Banks of Issue*, 299; C. Colton, *Henry Clay*, II., chs. iii.–iv.; Curtis, *Daniel Webster*, I., ch. xx.; Curtis, *James Buchanan*, I. 293, 409; Benton, *Thirty Years' View*, I. 373–400, 415, 458–62, 471–86, 658–65; E. G. Bourne, *History of Surplus Revenue of 1837*, p. 12; A. Johnston, *Removal of Deposits*, in Lalor's Cyclopedia, I. 199, 798; J. Parton, *Andrew Jackson*, I., xxi, III. 255, 493, 501; W. L. Royall, *Andrew Jackson and the Bank of U. S.;* Santvoord, *Chief Justices*, 552, 566; Sumner, *Andrew Jackson*, 345–356; Schurz, *Henry Clay*, II., chs. xv.–xviii.; L. G. Tyler, *Life of Tyler*, I., ch. xv.; S. Tyler, *Roger B. Taney;* G. Tucker, *History of U. S.*, IV., chs. xxviii.–xxix.; W. M. Gouge, *Short History of Banking and Paper Money in U. S.;* J. A. Hamilton, *Reminiscences;* H. von Holst, *Constitutional History of U. S.*, II. 52–79; A. Kendall, *Autobiography*, 378; Schouler, *History of U. S.*, IV., ch. xiv. sec. 1; Roosevelt, *Thomas H. Benton*, ch. vi.; Wise, *Seven Decades*, ch. vii.; Elliot, *Manual*, Pt. IV., ch. vi.; Young, *American Statesmen*, chs. xviii.–xix.; R. Hildreth, *Banks, Banking, and Paper Currencies*, ch. xxi.; Sumner, *History of Banking in the U. S.*, ch. xii.

SOURCES.—Gallatin, *Considerations on the Currency and Banking System of U. S.;* Webster, *Works*, III. 506–531, IV. 3–81, 200, 235, 297–300; *U. S. Statutes*, V. 52–56, 200, 296; Dunbar's *Laws*, 110, 116, 117, 123; *Statesman's Manual*, 837, 843; *Senate Doc.*, 1833–4, No. 17; *Ho. Exec. Doc.*, 1836–7, Nos. 118, 172; Niles, *Weekly Register*, XLV. 231, 236, 248, 258, 272; XLVI, 138, 355; XLIX. (see index, "Bank of U. S."); *Congressional Globe*, I.; Benton, *Abridgment of Debates*, XII., XIII.; J. Q. Adams, *Memoirs;* J. C. Calhoun, *Works*, II., III.; Clay, *Private Correspondence*, chs. ix.–x.; A. Kendall, *Autobiography*, ch. xiv.; N. Sargent, *Public Men and Events*, I. 253–277, 332–349; D. Mallory, *Life and Speeches of Henry Clay*, II.; W. MacDonald, *Select Documents*, 271, 289–303, 306–327, 329.

3. Expiration of the Charter and Last Efforts for a Bank.

BOOKS.—Benton, *Thirty Years' View*, II. 342; Von Holst, *Constitutional History of U. S.*, II. 199–218, 416–435; Sumner, *Andrew Jackson*, 352–71, 395–401, 426; Schurz, *Henry Clay*, II. 29,

51, 202-211, 256. Roosevelt, *Thomas H. Benton*, 123, 167, 225-7; Stevens, *Albert Gallatin*, 271-2; E. M. Shepard, *Martin Van Buren*, 252-4, 402.

SOURCES.—Dunbar's *Laws*, 272, 288; *Statesman's Manual*, 1248, 1260; *Ho. Exec. Doc.*, 1841-2, No. 20; Webster, *Works*, II. 134.

CHAPTER VIII.

THE SURPLUS REVENUE AND THE CRISIS OF 1837.

1. State Banks. Land Sales.

BOOKS.—H. C. Adams, *Public Debts*, 328; S. Sato, *Land Question*, J. H U. Studies, IV ; Stevens, *Albert Gallatin*, 271-2; Sumner, *Andrew Jackson*, 372-4, 377-80; Schurz, *Henry Clay*, II. 52, 115-9; Shepard, *Martin Van Buren*, 291-4, 308-312; Roosevelt, *Thomas H. Benton*, 137, 163; Pitkin, *Statistical View of U. S.*, ch x.; Sumner, *History of Banking in U. S* , ch. xiii.

SOURCES —Jackson's Messages, in *Presidents' Messages*, II 452, 514; III. 240.

2. The Distribution of the Surplus.

BOOKS.—Benton, *Thirty Years' View*, I 649-658, II. 36; E. G. Bourne, *History of Surplus Revenue of 1837;* Knox, *U. S Notes*, ch. xii.; Knox, in *Lalor's Cyclopedia*, III. 1032; Schurz, *Henry Clay*, II. ch. xix.; Sumner, *Andrew Jackson*, 382-387; Kearny, *Sketch of American Finances*, ch iv ; Sumner, *American Currency*, 115-131; C. Colton, *Henry Clay*, I., chs. xix -xx.; E. C. Mason, *Veto Power*, 83-94; Roosevelt, *Thomas H. Benton*, 129-137, 219-221; Shepard, *Martin Van Buren*, 300-2; Von Holst, *John C. Calhoun*, 150-1.

PERIODICALS.—C. F. Randolph, *Surplus Revenue*, Pol. Sci. Quart., III. 226; E. R Johnson, *River and Harbor Bills*, Annals, II. 782.

SOURCES,—*U. S. Statutes*, V. 52, 201; Dunbar's *Laws*, 110, 118; Webster, *Works*, IV. 252.

3. The Crisis of 1837, and the Specie Circular.

BOOKS.—Benton, *Thirty Years' View*, I. 676, 700, 706; II. 9-23; Bolles, *Financial History of U. S.*, II. 349; Conant, *History of Modern Banks of Issue*, 479-84; W. C. Ford, in *Lalor's Cyclopedia*, III. 474; Knox, *U. S. Notes*, ch. vi.; Schurz, *Henry Clay*, II., ch. xix.; Sumner, *Andrew Jackson*, 388-94, 450; Sumner, *History of American Currency*, 131-161; Sumner, *History of Banking in U. S.*, ch. xiv.; Hildreth, *Banks, Banking, and Paper Currencies*, chs. xxii.-xxv.; Shepard, *Martin Van Buren*, 304-23, 333-49, 370; Roosevelt, *Thomas H. Benton*, 139, 175-84; Lodge, *Daniel Webster*, 227.

SOURCES.—*U. S. Statutes*, V. 206; Dunbar's *Laws*, 120, 270, 271; *Statesman's Manual*, 1051; Niles' *Weekly Register*, L. 337, LII. 26; Webster, *Works*, IV. 265, 312; *Report of Secy. of Treas.*, 1837, 10, 16-20; *Sen. Doc.*, No. 2, 24th Cong., 2d sess., p. 96; W. MacDonald, *Select Documents*, 327.

4. The Coinage System.

BOOKS.—Bolles, *Financial History of U. S.*, II. 502-510; J. L. Laughlin, *History of Bimetallism in U. S.*, ch. iv.; McMaster, *History of the American People;* Sumner, *History of American Currency;* White, *Money and Banking;* Watson, *History of American Coinage;* DeKnight, *Currency and Loans;* G. L. Evans, *Illustrated History of U. S. Mint.*

SOURCES.—*U. S. Statutes*, IV. 699, V. 136; Dunbar's *Laws*, 234-236.

CHAPTER IX.

THE INDEPENDENT TREASURY AND THE CURRENCY, 1842-1860.

1. The Independent Treasury.

BOOKS.—Bolles, *Financial History of U. S.*, II. 351-8; D. Kinley, *The Independent Treasury of the U. S.;* Johnston, *The Independent Treasury*, in Lalor's Cyclopedia, II. 493; Knox, *U. S.*

Notes, chs. vi.–vii.; W. A. Scott, *Repudiation of State Debts;* Shepard, *Martin VanBuren*, 377; S. W. McCall, *Thaddeus Stevens*, 104–6.

SOURCES.—*U. S. Statutes*, V. 385, 439, IX. 59; Dunbar's *Laws*, 125, 132, 138; Benton, *Thirty Years' View*, II, chs. xxix., xli, lxiv., lxv., lxxx–lxxxv., xc., xci.; Webster, *Works*, IV. 200, 235, 312, 324, 402, 424; Woodbury, *Report of Secy. of Treas.*, Sen. Doc., 1837, No. 2; *Statesman's Manual*, 1051; MacDonald, *Select Documents*, 358–365; *Ho. Ex. Doc.*, 123, 27th Cong., 2d sess; Clay's *Speeches* (ed. 1844), II 279–303, 310–349, 384–405, 432–436; Benton's *Abridgment of Debates*, XV.

2. Treasury Notes and Loans.

BOOKS.—Bolles, *Financial History of U. S.*, II. 576–605; Knox, *U. S. Notes*, ch. vii.; Knox, in *Lalor's Cyclopedia*, III. 965–972; Bayley, *National Loans of U. S.*, Tenth Census of U. S., VII. 361, 434; Ross, *Sinking Funds*, 76; A. B. Hart, *Salmon P. Chase*, 216–220.

SOURCES—*U. S. Statutes*, V. 201, 614, IX. 39, 118; Dunbar's *Laws*, 118, 136; Spencer, *Report of Secy. of Treas.*, 1837, Sen. Doc. 1837, No. 2; Webster, *Works*, IV. 540; Report by Ways and Means Com., *Ho. Doc.*, 1843–4, No. 379.

3. Coinage Laws.

BOOKS.—Bolles, *Financial History of U. S.*, II., 511–517; Laughlin, *History of Bimetallism in U. S.*, ch. v.; Watson, *History of American Coinage*; White, *Money and Banking*.

SOURCES.—Walker, *Report of Secy. of Treas.*, 1848; *U. S. Statutes*, X. 160, 212; Dunbar's *Laws*, 238, 239.

4. State Finances. Repudiation of State Debts.

BOOKS.—W. A. Scott, *Repudiation of State Debts;* Roosevelt, *Thomas H. Benton*, 194–5, 220; Schurz, *Henry Clay*, II. 212; Sumner, *History of Banking in the U. S.* (see index, "Repudiation").

5. The Crisis of 1857.

BOOKS.—H. L. Baker, *History of Banks and Banking in U. S.;* Conant, *History of Modern Banks of Issue*, 492–6; Dunscomb,

Free Banking; W. M. Gouge, *History of U. S. Finances;* Raguet, *Treatise on Currency and Banking;* White, *Commercial Crises*, in Lalor's Cyclopedia, I. 523; S. W. McCall, *Thaddeus Stevens*, 104; Sumner, *History of Banking in the U. S.*, ch. xvi.

CHAPTER X.

THE FINANCES OF THE CIVIL WAR, 1861-1865.

1. The Financial Situation in 1861 and Chase's War Policy.

BOOKS.—H. C. Adams, *Public Debts*, 127-133; Appleton's *Annual Cyclopedia*, 1861, 295-9; Bayley, *History of National Loans*, Tenth Census, VII. 368, 442; Bolles, *Financial History of U. S.*, III., chs. i., ii.; J. W. Draper, *History of the American Civil War*, II. 552, 557, 575; A. B. Hart, *Salmon P. Chase*, 215-6, 220-9, 287-9; Knox, *History of Banking in the U. S.*, 220 ff.; Knox, *U. S. Notes*, chs. viii., ix.; H. McCulloch, *Men and Measures of Half a Century*, ch. xvi.; J. F. Rhodes, *History of the U. S*, III. 559 ff.; J. W. Schuckers, *Life of Chase*, chs. xxiv., xxv., xl.; D. A. Wells, *Theory and Practice of Taxation*, ch. i.; McCall, *Thaddeus Stevens*, 143-8, 163-5, 180-1; J. T. Morse, *Abraham Lincoln*, II. 170-1; Sumner, *History of Banking in U. S.*, 457 ff.

PERIODICALS.—C. W. Mitchell, *Suspension, 1861*, Journ. Pol. Econ., VII. 290.

SOURCES.—*Reports of the Secy. of Treas.*, 1860, 1861; John Sherman, *Recollections*, I. 251-4; R. J. Walker, *American Finances and Resources*.

2. The Suspension of Specie Payments and the Issue of Legal Tender Notes.

(1) The Necessity for Issues.

BOOKS.—C. F. Adams and F. A. Walker, *The Legal Tender Act*, in Na. Am. Rev., CX. 299; also in Adams' *Chapters of Erie*, 302-332; *Annual Cyclopedia*, 1861, 295-309; Bayley, *National Loans of U. S.*, Tenth Census, VII. 1, 369-385, 444-462; J. G. Blaine, *Twenty Years of Congress*, I., ch. xix.; Bolles, *Financial History of U. S.*,

III., chs. iii., iv., viii.; Bullock, *Monetary History*, ch. vii.; S. S. Cox, *Three Decades of Federal Legislation*, 129-136; DeKnight, *History of the Currency and Loans of our Country*, 77-99; Draper, *History of American Civil War*, II. 565 ff.; Hart, *S. P. Chase*, ch. ix.; Knox, *History of Banking*, ch. ix.; Knox, *U. S. Notes*, ch. ix.; also Lalor, III. 972; H. R. Linderman, *Money and Legal Tender in the U.S.;* S. W. McCall, *Thaddeus Stevens*, ch. ix.; S. Newcomb, *A Critical Examination of our Financial Policy during the Southern Rebellion;* Rhodes, *History of U. S.*, III. 561-572; IV. 237-8; Schuckers, *Life of Chase*, chs. xxvi.-xxix.; E. G. Spaulding, *History of Legal Tender Paper;* Sumner, *American Currency*, 189-215; F. W. Taussig, in Shaler's *United States*, II. 537-544; White, *Money and Banking*, 148-165.

PERIODICALS.—C. W. Mitchell, *The Suspension of Specie Payments*, 1861, J. P. E., VII. 289 ff.; *The Greenback in Congress*, Sound Currency, III., No. 4; *Bankers' Magazine*, 1861-2, 453 ff.; 1863, 394-8, 398, 402, 406; R. M. Breckenridge, *The Demand Notes of 1861*, Sound Currency, V. 389, 444; Hunt's *Merchants' Magazine*, 1861-2.

SOURCES.—Acts in *U. S. Statutes*, XII. 218, 259, 345, 532, 709; in Dunbar's *Laws*, 160, 163, 167, 173, 193; in *Monetary Commission Report* 389-417, 501; *U. S. Congressional Globe*, 1861-2, 663, 687, 762, 767; Chas. Sumner, *Works*, VI. 319-345.

(ii) Constitutionality.

BOOKS.—G. Bancroft, *A Plea for the Constitution;* also in Sound Currency, V. 161-176; Bolles, *Financial History of U. S.*, III., Bk. II., ch. i.; Hart, *S. P. Chase*, ch. xv.; E. J. James, *Legal Tender Decisions*, Pub. Am. Econ. Assn., III. 49-80, 207; Knox, *U. S. Notes*, ch. xi., 193 ff. (Decisions of U. S. Court); Madison, in Elliot's *Debates*, V. 435; S. F. Miller, *Lectures on the Constitution*, 135-144; Schuckers, *Life of Chase*, I., ch. xxviii.; J. B. Thayer, in *Harvard Law Review* (May, 1887), I. 79; C. F. Adams, *Chapters of Erie*, 302-332; Blaine, *Twenty Years of Congress*, I., ch. xix.; Linderman, *Money and Legal Tender in U. S.;* McCall, *Thaddeus Stevens*, ch. ix.; Rhodes, *History of U. S.*, III. 561, IV. 237; Shaler, *United States*, II. 537; White, *Money and Banking*, 148-165.

SOURCES.—Gallatin, *Writings*, III. 235; Chas. Sumner, *Works*, VI. 319-345; J. B. Thayer, *Cases on Constitutional Law*, 2222, 2237, 2255; *U. S. Supreme Court Reports*; 8 Wallace 603; 12 Wallace 457; 110 U. S. 421; Webster, *Works*, IV. 270.

(iii) Effect on the Cost of the War and on the Nation.

BOOKS.—Appleton's *Annual Cyclopedia*, 1862, 468–472; 1863, 407–8, 412–3; Blaine, *Twenty Years in Congress*, I. 428–9; Bolles, *Financial History of U. S.*, III., chs. viii., xiii.; *Monetary Commission Report*, 445, 479, 562; Shuckers, *Life of Chase*, 356–362, 401; White, *Money and Banking*, 160–5, 174 ff.; Hart, *Salmon P. Chase*, 283–5.

PERIODICALS.—H. C. Adams, *American War Financiering*, Pol. Sci. Quart., I.; C. W. Mitchell, *Greenbacks and the Cost of the Civil War*, Journ. Pol. Econ., V. 117; Mitchell, *Value of Greenbacks during the Civil War*, Journ. Pol. Econ., VI. 139; Moses, *Legal Tender Notes in California*, Quart. Journ. Econ., VII. 1; Powers, *The Greenback in War*, Pol. Sci. Quart., II.

3. Loans.

BOOKS.—H. C. Adams, *Public Debts*, 167–8; *Annual Cyclopedia*, 1861–1865 (see under "Finance," 1863, 260–6); Bayley, *National Loans of U. S.*, Tenth Census, VII. Pt. 1, 369–388, 444–462; Blaine, *Twenty Years in Congress*, II., ch. xiii.; Bolles, *Financial History of U. S.*, III., chs. ii., iii., vi.; DeKnight, *Currency and Loans*, 77–99; Draper, *History of American Civil War*, II. 557 ff.; III, 491–7; Hart, *S. P. Chase*, 241–3; Rhodes, *History of U. S.*, IV. 238, 427–8; Schuckers, *Life of Chase*, 220–1, 224–8, 338–355; Ross, *Sinking Funds*, Pub. Am. Econ. Ass'n, VII. 389; Gibbons, *The U. S. Debt and Taxation*.

4. National Banks.

BOOKS.—Appleton's *Annual Cyclopedia*, 1863, 1864 (see under "National Banks"); Blaine, *Twenty Years in Congress*, I. 470–487; Bolles, *Financial History of U. S.*, III., ch. xi.; Cox, *Three Decades of Federal Legislation*, 141–4; Dunbar, *Theory and History of Banking*, ch. viii.; Hart, *S. P. Chase*, ch. xi.; Knox, *History of Banking*, chs. vii., ix., xiv., xv., xviii.; H. McCulloch, *Men and Measures of Half a Century*, chs. xv., xvi., xvii.; *Monetary Commission Report*, 197–210; Schuckers, *Life of Chase*, I., chs. xxxi.-xxxiii.; Sumner, *History of Banking in U. S.*, ch. xvii.

PERIODICALS.—J. W. Million, *The Debate on the National Bank Act of 1863*, Journ. Pol. Econ., II. 251.

SOURCES.—Acts in *U. S. Statutes*, VII. 665, XIII. 99, 469,

XVIII. 296, XXII. 162; in Dunbar's *Laws*, 171, 178, 198, 214, 219; in *Monetary Commission Report*, 505, 508, 511, 517; Knox, *Comptroller's Report*, 1876, 137, 149; *Report of Secy. of Treas.*, 1862, 11–21; 1863, 55; *U. S. Congressional Globe*, 1862–3, 384, 840, 869; Chas. Sumner, *Works*, VIII. 419 ff.

5. Revenue Measures.

BOOKS.—Appleton's *Annual Cyclopedia*, 1861, 296, 301, 671–5; 1862, 460–1; 1863, 406; 1864, 1865, under "Finance"; Blaine, *Twenty Years in Congress*, I. 399, 429–434, 480, 543–4; Bolles, *Financial History of U. S.*, III., chs. ii., ix., x., xii.; Cox, *Three Decades of Federal Legislation*, 137; W. C. Ford, *The Income Tax*, Lalor's Encyclopedia, II. 488–90; Ford, *Internal Revenue*, Lalor's Encyclopedia, II. 576; Hart, *S. P. Chase*, 233–249; F. C. Howe, *Taxation in the U. S. under the Internal Revenue System;* McCall, *Thaddeus Stevens* ch. x.; Schuckers, *Life of Chase*, 222–4, 312 ff, 330–337; Taussig, *The Tariff History of U. S.*, 155–175; D. A. Wells, *Distilled Spirits*, in Lalor's Encyclopedia, I. 809; D. A. Wells, *Theory and Practice of Taxation*, ch. i.; Wells, *Practical Economics;* Gould and Tucker, *The Federal Income Tax Explained;* von Hock, *Die Finanzen uud Finanzgeschichte der Vereinigten Staaten von Amerika.*

PERIODICALS.—Dunbar, *Direct Tax of 1861*, Quart. Journ. Econ. III. 436; J. A. Hill, *The Civil War Income Tax*, Quart. Journ. Econ., VIII. 416, 491; F. C. Howe, *Federal Revenues and the Income Tax*, Annals, IV. 557.

SOURCES.—Acts in *U. S. Statutes*, XII. 294 (secs. 8–48), 432; XIII. 223, 469; *Ho. Exec. Doc.*, 1884–5, No. 4 (internal revenue report); *Report of Secy. of Treas.*, 1883, 163.

6. The Finances of the Confederacy.

BOOKS.—Appleton's *Annual Cyclopedia*, 1861–5 (see index, "Finance" and "Confederacy"); Draper, *History of American Civil War*, III. 456; E. A. Pollard, *The Lost Cause*, 416, 650; White, *Money and Banking*, 166–174; J. C. Schwab, *Financial and Industrial History of the South during the Civil War.*

PERIODICALS.—J. C. Schwab, *The Finances of the Confederacy*, Pol. Sci. Quart., 1892; Schwab, *Confederate Foreign Loans*, Yale Rev., I. 175; Schwab, *The Financier of the Confederate States*, Yale Rev., II. 228.